LifeWork

RICK SARKISIAN, PH.D.

LifeWork

Finding Your Purpose in Life

IGNATIUS PRESS

Cover art by Jim Goold

© 1997 Ignatius Press, San Francisco
All rights reserved
ISBN 978-0-89870-636-9
Library of Congress catalogue number 97–70812
Printed in the United States of America ∞

This book is dedicated in loving memory to my father who passed from this world when I was fifteen years of age. He provided much love to our family, and I will be forever grateful for the seeds of my Catholic faith that Dad planted in great abundance.

Contents

Illustrations

Cover art and illustrations by Jim Goold: iii, xi, 1,
3, 5, 6, 7, 10, 12, 13, 15, 16, 17, 19, 20, 21, 23,
25, 27, 28, 31, 32, 33, 35, 37, 39, 40, 41, 43, 44,
45, 46, 49, 50, 52, 53, 54, 57, 60, 61, 63, 64, 72,
75, 76, 77, 78, 79, 80, 81, 82, 83, 84, 86, 87, 91,
92, 93, 95, 96, 98, 99, 106, 107, 109, 113

Photographs:

Catholic News Service: 7, 29, 30

Legionaries of Christ: 60, 112

Oblates of St. Joseph: 31

Acknowledgments

I am especially grateful to my good friend Christopher Knuffke of Catholic Truth International, who has been such a close collaborator on this project.

My gratitude also extends to my cousin Fr. Larry Toschi of the Oblates of St. Joseph for his encouragement and doctrinal review.

My family has also been a wonderful source of inspiration for this book. My wife and five beautiful children continue to be a reflection of my chosen vocation and the source of immeasurable joy. They bring Jesus into my heart each day.

Also thanks to Jim Goold for his outstanding artistic contributions and to Phebe Wahl for her great layout skills and ongoing guidance in developing the style of the book.

The author wishes gratefully to acknowledge the use of four important publications from the U.S. Department of Labor: *Exploring Careers,* Bulletin 2001, 1979 (Bureau of Labor Statistics); the *Dictionary of Occupational Titles,* 4th ed., revised 1991; the *Guide for Occupational Exploration,* 1979; and the *Occupational Outlook Handbook,* 1996–1997 edition. Portions of these publications were used in the career section of chapter 4.

Finally, I want to thank Rogationist Father Rodolfo D'Agostino, editor of VOCATIONS *and Prayer Magazine.* His support has been one of those "signs" discussed later in this book.

*For everything
there is a season,
and a time for every
matter under heaven.*

(Ecclesiastes 3:1)

Introduction

Have you ever asked:
"Who am I?
Where am I going and how do I get there?
What is my purpose in life?"

"As each has received a gift, employ it for one another, as good stewards of God's varied grace." (1 Peter 4:10)

God is calling each of us to live a life of holiness, joy, and great peace, resting in His merciful love and comforting presence. God is calling us to a unique, personal vocation and mission, a way to follow Jesus throughout our life, using the gifts, talents, and skills He has provided.

Life passes from one beginning to other beginnings, from commitments and decisions to further commitments. We therefore need to seek the grace to know God's will and in so knowing to serve Him above all things. Then our reward will be a true, lasting **joy**, not the fleeting experience of "pleasure" or "happiness".

How to Use This Book

LifeWork: Finding Your Purpose in Life is a tool for discovering the unique, personal plan God has for our life. Each of us is called to live a life of holiness, peace, and joy—to serve Him in our unique way with the particular gifts, talents, and skills He has provided us.

A **tree** is used to illustrate the process of responding to Christ's call to follow Him.

The parts of the tree—the roots, trunk, limbs, branches, leaves, and fruit—each play an important role in this process. In nature, the roots anchor the tree in the ground, absorb water, and dissolve minerals necessary for growth. The trunk and branches carry sap, a substance that contains the ingredients vital for growth and a healthy tree. The branches also hold the leaves in the sunlight, the source of all its life and energy. The leaves take carbon dioxide out of the atmosphere and give back oxygen, purifying the air. Finally the fruit develops—the outcome of the process.

So in our lives, the process of responding to Christ's call to follow Him requires a foundation or an anchor. We need a strong anchor in order to grow in holiness, making commitments to activities and situations that cultivate our unique way to follow Jesus Christ. Carrying out God's plan for our life takes many forms, including the branch of career involvement in addition to other roles in God's family and the world. Finally, we should look for the fruit, evidence that we are growing in grace, filling our life with Jesus and the fullness of the Holy Spirit.

Chapter by chapter, page by page, *LifeWork: Finding Your Purpose in Life* will guide you in the process of discovering the unique, personal plan God has for your life. Hear God's call and follow Him. Whatever your state, whether you are called to marriage, the priesthood, or consecrated life, remain single, or are still undecided about your personal vocation, whether you are a student, waitress, welder, doctor, accountant, or teacher, He wants you to grow in knowledge and love of Him. Learn to hear His call, and respond with a firm and unwavering "Yes".

1
The Roots

The Roots before the Fruit

"He is like a tree planted by streams of water, that yields its fruit in its season. . . ."

(Psalm 1:3)

". . . a branch shall grow out of his roots." (Isaiah 11:1)

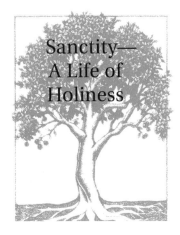

Sanctity—
A Life of
Holiness

A seed becomes a healthy plant if it is provided with good soil, food, and sunlight. A seed of faith is planted in baptism.

The roots of a young sprout grow and provide a strong foundation for the much larger tree that will be seen in years to come. These roots represent the sanctity (holiness) in your life as a member of Christ's Body.

". . . if the root is holy, so are the branches." (Romans 11:16)

What Is Holiness?

It is simply dedicating yourself to God and living your life in His presence. It is seeing Him in all things. It is living a life of faith, hope, and love. It is seeing others as Jesus sees them. This life of grace is fostered by the sacraments, beginning with baptism and nourished through the Eucharist, which helps you to become holy in preparation for eternal life.

What Is Grace?

Grace is divine assistance to help you grow closer to God. A life of grace transforms the believer into one who has developed a greater and ever-increasing knowledge and love of God and love of others through Him. Grace also heals sin, helps in time of need, and guides you on the path to salvation and eternity with God.

You Can Be a Saint!

God asks each of us to grow in holiness and grace and to become saints. Throughout history, He has often chosen **very ordinary people** to do His work, people from all walks of life, people who became great saints!

Roots

The soil that holds the roots is like your faith. If the soil is rich and well fed, the roots will grow and become stronger. If the soil is dry and unfertilized, the roots will not grow and may become dormant or die. The soil must be **fed** for a tree to reach maturity and become what it is meant to be. A strong faith leads to strong roots.

Some trees remain small while the roots spread out and become well established in the soil. Then, significant growth occurs, and the tree becomes very tall.

Strength

"Feeding the roots" means making the soil moist and rich, letting the roots grow. The roots can then absorb more and more food from the soil and provide *strength* to the trunk, limbs, and branches of the tree.

Food for faith can be prayer, reading Scripture, receiving the sacraments (especially confession and Holy Communion), and involvement in Church activities.

"... consider your call. ..."
(1 Corinthians 1:26)

Prayer is a way to keep your faith strong and well anchored. **You don't want to blow over when a storm comes!**

Roots are very important.

God's call and direction in their lives. They have given us real-life examples of how God works in shaping the lives of His followers.

Like a mirror, saints reflected the image of God. **So can you!** The saints are role models for what you do with your time on earth. Like them, you are called to a life that reflects the presence of God.

A Mirror Image

The saints are great examples of lay people, priests, religious brothers or sisters who have followed

Tough Times

The saints show you ways to **respond** to God and how to **prevail** when you face difficult or confusing times in your life. The **weeds** (sin) in your life choke out growth and so require constant vigilance. **Rip** them out by the roots when they pop up from the ground! Confession can help greatly, providing God's grace to wipe out sin.

When you pray, you can listen for the will of God. If you are not listening for His call, it will be very difficult to hear it, especially

Through prayer you can listen for the will of God.

because of the many daily distractions that can drown out His voice.

Your daily struggles can be viewed, not so much as **problems**, but as **opportunities** to strengthen the roots, especially if you are following Christ, walking with Him. For example, if you are having difficulty in a relationship with someone, look on the situation as a way to grow closer to God through prayer, and let Him take over. The growth of the roots help all the other parts of the tree become larger, stronger, and better defined.

Your growth in holiness (sanctity) depends a lot on faith and how you obtain spiritual food in your daily life. The sacraments, especially regular confession (at least monthly) and Holy Communion, are wonderful paths to sanctity and to receiving God's **grace**.

Knowing God's Will

In these pages, you will explore some ways in which you can grow in the knowledge of how God works in your life. Knowing God's will naturally involves the Holy Spirit, who will guide you along the right paths as you journey through life.

The starting point is prayer, being open to your **vocation** (called by God) and **mission** in life (sent by God).

> "So Jesus answered them, 'My teaching is not mine, but his who sent me; if any man's will is to do his will, he shall know whether the teaching is from God or whether I am speaking on my own authority.'"
> (John 7:16–17)

God has given you the gifts of intellect and free will. By the light of faith, you can learn to follow the road signs that are found along the way. When you pray the Our Father, you say, "Thy will be done. . . ." **His will** includes the **free will** that has been given to you and seen throughout biblical history, such as the free will of the apostles to follow Jesus.

There are often signs from God that help you understand His will. Church teaching, prayer, and Scripture can help you in your discernment. You should also consider moral issues (right and wrong), the question of how **best** to use the time God has given you, and whether or not your choices would bring glory to Him.

These signs, coupled with your ability to reason and exercise free will, and the situations of your life, should blend together, making a clear statement that **yes**, this is a wise, God-loving choice that is being made.

A good way to know if you are on the right track in your decisions is to look for the **fruits** of the Spirit (see chapter 5). Another way is to remember what the Church has taught regarding your **purpose** in life:

To know Him

To **know** God well, you must **pray daily**.

To love Him

To **love** God involves knowing Him well and making your life a gift to Him. You must love God **above all things**.

To serve Him

To **serve** God, you must bring glory to Him by working well, praying well, and living out your vocation and mission as one of His adopted children.

Prayer

Consistent, daily prayer is very important in discovering God's will in your life. Set aside a specific time each day for prayer. Start with at least ten to fifteen minutes, increasing the time with God as needed when your conversation with Him covers more aspects of your life. Find a spot that will serve as your place for prayer—a specific room, chair, or other setting. Then begin by doing the following:

Praising

God for His majesty, holiness, and glory

Reading

Scripture

Examining

your conscience and repenting of any wrongdoing

Asking

> God to help in your needs or the needs of others

Thanking

> God for the blessings He gives, offering each day to Him

St. Thérèse of the Child Jesus   "The Little Flower"

Thérèse was born in France in 1873. Often called "The Little Flower", she wanted to be a saint from an early age. She experienced a profound conversion on Christmas Day at age thirteen and entered a Carmelite convent at age fifteen. She wrote: "The good God would not inspire unattainable desires. I may then, in spite of my littleness, aspire to holiness. I cannot make myself greater; I must bear with myself just as I am with all my imperfections."

She prayed much and performed ordinary tasks like scrubbing, washing, cooking, and sewing. Regarding God's call in her life, she said, "I saw that all vocations are summed up in Love, and Love

October 1

is all in all." Her spiritual autobiography, *The Story of a Soul,* is a beautiful look into her remarkable interior life. As Pope Pius XI said, "She became holy without going beyond the ordinary circumstances of life."

Summary

Roots firmly anchor the tree and are an important foundation for everything that grows from a seed. Similarly, the grace and holiness in your life begin with a rich faith (like good soil) that allows the roots to flourish and grow, becoming well established in God's field and eventually bearing fruit for a rich harvest.

Reflections

How can you know God better? Let's look at some ways to do that.

Prayer

I will continue doing the following:

I will start doing the following:

Scripture and Church teaching

I will continue doing the following:

I will start doing the following:

Sacraments

(especially confession and Holy Communion)

I will continue doing the following:

I will start doing the following:

God's will is often revealed in the signs around us. How have you seen His will recently?

Prayer

Lord Jesus, Praised be Your holy Name!
Open my ears to Your call, and teach me to
follow Your will throughout my life. Teach
me to seek You in all things and to find You
in all that I do. Amen.

Remember

**Prayer, sacraments, and Scripture are
spiritual food. Strong roots make for a
strong tree.**

2
The Trunk

The Trunk—
Growing in Holiness

"Either make the tree good, and its fruit good; or make the tree bad, and its fruit bad; for the tree is known by its fruit." (Matthew 12:33)

Pillar of Strength

As the tree grows from the seed, so you grow from baptism into an involved member of the Church (His Body). The **trunk** represents our **universal vocation and call** to grow in holiness and become united with God.

A Family Affair

We are a family—God's family—in communion with the saints of this earth and the saints who have passed from this earth into eternal life. We are like a forest of trees. The work of God is so clearly shown in the history of the Church through the lives of so many saints. God's work has also been reflected in our own time by dedicated men and women such as Pope John Paul II and Mother Teresa of Calcutta.

As you travel the journey toward becoming saints (yes, you are all called to become saints), remember that holiness can often be achieved in the ordinary circumstances of life. "Holiness in the ordinary" is part of the spiritual life followed by the Oblates of St. Joseph, a religious order founded by Blessed Joseph Marello in Italy.

It is not essential that you accomplish great things to be holy. You can seek holiness in the humdrum, in the day-to-day activities that fill your life, offering the little things and the big things to the Lord in a way that mirrors His presence. Mother Teresa has spoken of **"little acts of love"** as we go through life.

The Holy Spirit

The Holy Spirit works in our lives as sap works in the life of the tree.

Sap brings food and nourishment **for growth, flowing up** from the roots and trunk into the limbs and branches. Soon, the tree bears fruit!

We Are the Branches

In the parable about the vine and the branches (John 15:1–8), Jesus describes our lives as "branches", abiding or resting in Him. As branches, we take form, length, and shape. We draw life from the vine and will eventually bear fruit. If we separate ourselves from the vine, we no longer receive life and thus become dead wood.

". . . be like a fruitful vine within your house. . . ." (Psalm 128:3)

But we are also like a vine, which is rooted in faith and becomes stronger as the roots grow stronger. God is the gardener, the One who tends the vine. As you pray and receive the sacraments and the outpouring of His grace, your roots become firmly established in the soil.

God owns the vineyard, and you therefore belong to Him. You are planted on an earthly farm, quite distant from your heavenly home, yet the way you grow and the fruit you bear will be harvested by the Lord for heaven's banquet.

The Not-So-Secret Garden

You are like a tree in God's garden. He is creator of the seed that has grown into a tree. Like other plants, you are subject to storms, disease, drought, and other outside forces, yet you never stop being a tree, His tree. If you attempt to be something else, you betray your real identity.

Your universal vocation to be holy is followed by your **unique personal vocation**, God's call to serve Him in a particular state of life, such as marriage, the priesthood, or consecrated life, and in other ways that will be explored shortly.

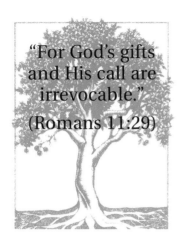

> "For God's gifts and His call are irrevocable."
> (Romans 11:29)

Serious Business

To be serious about your commitment to follow Christ means making sure He is your top priority—above everything else in your life.

What is God's plan for my life?

Remember the young man in the Gospels who asked Jesus, *"What must I do to inherit eternal life?"* Pope John Paul II teaches that he was asking, *"What must I do so that my life may have meaning?"* *"What is God's plan for my life?"* *"What is His will?"* Jesus responds with *"Follow me."* You, like the young man, are therefore called to follow Jesus.

"Follow me . . ." (Matthew 4:19)

God's Call

To hear God's call is to understand His purpose for your life. It is being what God wants you to be. His call may be as gentle as a summer evening's breeze.

Sometimes God will call in a very specific way, and at other times, He will be more general. For example, He may call someone to perform a very specific activity in a particular setting, such as being a Youth Director at a particular parish.

"We know that in everything God works for good with those who love him, who are called according to his purpose." (Romans 8:28)

In other instances, He may just provide a gentle nudge in a general direction, then guide us through our prayerful choices. For example, a man may be called to the priesthood, but the calling to a specific religious order may occur at a later time once he has explored various possibilities.

Regardless of whether the call is specific or general, God is inviting us to cooperate with Him.

Called by Name

God calls you by name in a way that emphasizes your unique identity as His child. Think of your brothers, sisters, cousins, or parents. Each is uniquely different, one

He knows you

"Before I formed you in the womb, I knew you, and before you were born, I consecrated you; I appointed you a prophet to the nations." (Jeremiah 1:5)

He calls you

"But now thus says the Lord, he who created you, O Jacob, he who formed you, O Israel: 'Fear not, for I have redeemed you; **I have called you by name, you are mine.'** " (Isaiah 43:1)

from the other, and each has a special set of characteristics that create his identity, who he is. God calls you to a specific plan that will bring great fulfillment to your life and allow you to achieve a mature partnership with Jesus Christ.

You are chosen, according to God's purpose, to a vocation (state of life) and to a specific mission. He consecrates you (sets you apart) for this purpose so that you can walk along the path of holy living into eternity.

"Make me to know thy ways, O Lord; teach me thy paths. Lead me in thy truth, and teach me, for thou art the God of my salvation; for thee I wait all the day long." (Psalm 25:4–5)

Are you willing to surrender, to turn your life over to Jesus Christ? If you put Him in charge, He will guide you through the dense forest of many paths and many forks in the road. He will sometimes point His finger to a very clear way chosen for you. At other times, He will extend His hand outward and gesture toward a more general direction allowing further choices along the way.

For example, someone called to the general vocation of marriage may not be called immediately to marry a specific person. Eventually, however, he may meet the specific person, also chosen by God, whom he is called to marry. Thus, the general state-of-life choice for marriage becomes a more specific vocation when the two meet according to God's purpose and vow a life of faithfulness together.

"And I am sure that he who began a good work in you will bring it to completion at the day of Jesus Christ." (Philippians 1:6)

Cooperation with God

The Father, Son, and Holy Spirit are always present, working directly with each choice, each action, each outcome as life moves forward. As you cooperate with God in exercising free will, He remains present, interacting with you as you respond to His will.

Each calling is a highly personalized opportunity to grow in holiness and to serve others. Yet all the details of His call may not be visible when His will is first discovered. By receiving a continued outpouring of His grace, you gradually work out the details, so to speak, with God, who often broadens your horizons and enlarges your perspective. It is not unusual for many of these "details" about your personal vocation to be a great surprise.

"You, therefore, must be perfect, as your heavenly Father is perfect."
(Matthew 5:48)

God's will is perceived by a combination of interior factors (desires, intuition, common sense, knowledge of right and wrong) and external forces (other people, circumstances, opportunities that arise). As you attempt to sort out God's will from other influences in your life, you will be guided by the Holy Spirit. Even then, you might make mistakes and wrong choices, yet the Lord will

"We know that in everything God works for good with those who love him, who are called according to his purpose." (Romans 8:28)

Memorize
Romans 8:28

never let you down. He will be there to turn your errors into great goodness.

God's will for you is His purpose and destiny for your life. His call to a personal vocation is a call for you to discover **who you are to become** in His great plan for your life and in what ways you are to serve Him. He also reveals how you can live out this unique, one-of-a-kind life. You have been **chosen** out of His incredibly **vast** love, and you are **called** to choose and love God in return.

The Beatitudes

The Beatitudes are of great value in knowing God's will in your daily life. They reflect your **universal** vocation in the Church and lay the foundation for your **personal** vocation.

Blessed are the poor in spirit,

>   for theirs is the kingdom of heaven.

Blessed are those who mourn,

>   for they shall be comforted.

Blessed are the meek,

>   for they shall inherit the earth.

Blessed are those who hunger and thirst for righteousness,

>   for they shall be satisfied.

Blessed are the merciful,

>   for they shall obtain mercy.

Blessed are the pure in heart,

>   for they shall see God.

Blessed are the peacemakers,

>   for they shall be called sons of God.

Blessed are those who are persecuted for righteousness' sake,

>   for theirs is the kingdom of heaven. Blessed are you when men revile you and persecute you and utter all kinds of evil against you falsely on my account. Rejoice and be glad, for your reward is great in heaven, for so men persecuted the prophets who were before you.

>   (Matthew 5:3–12)

St. Dominic Savio

A Boy Saint

Dominic heard God's call at an early age. He was attending daily Mass and serving at the altar by the age of five. At age seven, he made his first Holy Communion and wrote four promises in a little book that he often reread:

I will go often to confession, and I will go to Holy Communion as often as I am allowed.

I will try to give Sundays and holy days completely to God.

My best friends will be Jesus and Mary.

Death, but not sin.

May 6

At age twelve, he became a student at St. John Bosco's school and expressed his wish to become a priest.

He was loved by his schoolmates for his cheerful and kind disposition and was very devoted to the Eucharist. He studied hard and had a love of prayer. Because of poor health, he returned home after two years of school. He died at age fourteen on March 9, 1857. His words were: "What a beautiful thing I see."

Pope St. Pius X called Dominic a true model for the youth of our times. The two miracles accepted for his beatification involved teenagers!

Summary

In this second chapter, we looked at the trunk as the natural outgrowth of the seed and at the call to holiness from baptism onward. By trusting in God and seeking Him **above** all things and **in** all things, we will grow **strong and tall.**

Reflections

My baptism date was:

How have the "roots" and "trunk" grown since my baptism?

How do I experience the Holy Spirit's presence in my life now?

Prayer

O Holy Spirit, flow into my life and through all my decisions. Let me abide in the true vine, Christ, and seek the will of God in all the choices I face in life. Jesus, I trust in You. Amen.

Remember

Let the Holy Spirit flow through your life; trust and abide in Jesus each day. Be on alert for the enemy, Satan.

3
The Limbs

The Limbs—
Your Vocation

From one beginning to another, you make commitments to activities and situations that cultivate your personal vocation, your unique way to follow Jesus Christ.

W e are all laborers in the vineyard, each of us as God's child using the gifts, talents, and abilities He has given to us. We are each unique members of God's family, yet we all work in the one and same vineyard of life. Whether we are called to the priesthood, marriage, or consecrated life, we join together in service to God for the Church.

". . . the harvest is plentiful, but the laborers are few; pray therefore the Lord of the harvest to send out laborers into his harvest." (Luke 10:2)

Living Plants

Devotion is your commitment to serving God, dedicating yourself fully to His service in a very personal way. The building blocks of this devotion are **prayer** and **worship.**

St. Francis de Sales tells us:

"In creation God commanded the plants to bring forth their fruits, each one after its kind. So does He command all Christians, who are the living plants of His Church, to bring forth the fruits of devotion, each according to his character and vocation."

St. Francis de Sales also explains that devotion is shown in different ways by different people and must be part of every believer's life, whether one is a soldier, prince, mechanic, laborer; single or married.

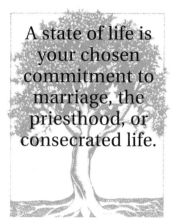

A state of life is your chosen commitment to marriage, the priesthood, or consecrated life.

States of Life

Your **personal vocation** may involve following God's call to a particular state of life, such as:

Marriage

A married couple is a man and a woman who vow faithfulness to each other through the sacrament of marriage.

Priesthood

A priest may be a man who serves as diocesan priest (with promises of chastity and obedience to his bishop) or a religious order priest (with vows of chastity, poverty, and obedience to the superiors of his congregation).

Consecrated Life

A consecrated person (religious) is one who joins a religious order as brother or sister (with vows of chastity, poverty, and obedience to his or her congregation). A single person taking the vow of perpetual chastity is also living a consecrated life.

Permanent Diaconate

A deacon is a single or married man called to ordained ministry to assist diocesan priests and the bishop(s).

For more information about states of life, please see "Vocations in the Catholic Church" (page 109).

Your personal vocation is not just a commitment to a state of life. It is a commitment to follow God's lead in **all** aspects of your life.

" '. . . and the two shall become one.' So they are no longer two but one." (Mark 10:8)

Being Single

All persons start out in life single. Some remain single for a while as they seek God's call and discover their vocation in marriage. Even then, the vocation of marriage must be lived out by meeting someone of the opposite sex who also is called to this vocation.

Others may realize God's call to the priesthood and religious life. Still others may remain in a "pre-vocation" state while trying to understand the will of God and how they are to serve Him.

After understanding God's call to a particular state of life, one must decide to accept His will. And in choosing a spouse, the potential marriage partner must also decide whether or not to accept this choice.

Chastity is an important virtue common to all vocations and also applies to single persons in a prevocation state (those seeking God's will for their life). Chastity involves the unity between bodily and spiritual existence to which all baptized persons are called, in accordance with their particular states of life. Some are called to

vow perpetual chastity, giving themselves completely to God. Others who marry or remain single are called to live a chaste life in keeping with the teachings of the Church.

Consecration—What Is It?

Consecration can involve committing yourself to God exclusively for His service, such as by being a priest, religious order brother or sister, or consecrated single person. Such a vocation involves a vow or promise. Interestingly, a man and woman are also consecrated in the marriage sacrament: as individuals to each other and to God as a united couple.

Consecration is the dedication of oneself to serving God. Each Catholic is consecrated to God by the sacraments of baptism and confirmation.

Consecration also means to make something sacred, such as changing bread and wine into the Body and Blood of Christ (Eucharist) at the Mass. What is consecrated is set apart.

A single person who thinks about the consecrated life may be drawn toward a vowed, celibate life and perhaps to a specific commitment to the religious life as a priest, brother, or sister. However, being single may also allow one to continue seeking God's will in a vocation to marriage. Regardless, God continues to respond to the single person's prayers, internal thoughts and desires, and to work through external circumstances, so that His plan can be discovered.

Making a Commitment

When you receive the sacrament of orders or matrimony or make vows in religious life, you make an unbreakable, life-long commitment to God for the state of life He has called you to, and you acknowledge your identity as God's child, like a limb abiding in the trunk of the tree. You want to allow the Holy Spirit to work in your life so that you may bear much fruit.

Although a state-of-life commitment is a major decision, it is also the beginning of a **process** in which God continues to reveal His will and guidance. This may involve more decisions along the way.

In discovering, accepting, and making a commitment to your personal vocation, you then enter a life-long process of listening for God's call. You acknowledge your God-given talents, skills, and abilities as **gifts** and follow His lead in **accepting** them to perform various tasks. You

Coming and Going

You have seen how vocation involves **coming** to God—being planted in His soil. You will see how **mission** involves working for God and His kingdom and so living out your personal vocation in the process. Part of your mission may be the choice of career that will be discussed in chapter 4.

". . . the branch cannot bear fruit by itself." (John 15:4)

have a set of unique gifts and tasks that make up your special way of doing the will of the Father.

Great Faith

The best, all-time example of vocation and state of life is found in the Holy Family (Jesus, Mary, and Joseph). For example, St. Joseph is the just man who affirmed his vocation through betrothal and marriage to Mary and followed his mission as **guardian of the Redeemer** while working as a craftsman. It is also significant that God chose a family as the way to bring His Son to us. It is in the family that we can begin to consider our vocation, state of life, and mission.

Your mission may also involve work within the Church, including spreading the gospel message and helping others come to Christ. For Catholics, vocation means hearing God's call to follow Christ in a specific way throughout life and responding to this divine message each time it is heard.

Within the image of a tree you can see our Lord as gardener and seed planter and the Holy Spirit as the life-giving sap that flows into the limbs and branches to bear fruit.

Peeling Onions

Once decisions are made regarding your personal vocation and mission, God continues to reveal His will, increasing your knowledge of Him. These kinds of decisions usually involve further unfolding (like peeling an onion, layer by layer). Finding your personal vocation is not a one-time discovery but needs to be lived out, all the while listening for and accepting God's on-going guidance.

St. Joseph   A Humble, Profound Life

St. Joseph heard God's call and responded with obedience and generosity. He was chosen among all men by God to be chaste husband to Mary and foster-father to Jesus, guiding the Christ Child in His formative years. His life was spent at work, prayer, and dedication to support and protect Jesus and Mary.

His life was filled with humility, modesty, quietness, and complete, loving acceptance of God's will. He is a strong example of hearing God's call and following His will in marriage, family, and work (all part of his personal vocation and mission).

March 19

Summary

In the third chapter, we considered your personal vocation, your unique way to follow Jesus. Your commitment to a state of life, such as marriage or the priesthood, will require further unfolding—additional commitments and decisions stemming from the original commitment. For example, entering marriage is only the beginning of many other commitments, such as to children, aging parents, parish life, and so forth. Newer commitments can also strengthen earlier choices.

A state of life, vowed or consecrated before God, is a commitment.

The largest commitments in your personal vocation may involve a state of life consecrated by a sacrament or vows, followed by many smaller commitments concerning work, service to the community, leisure, and recreational pursuits.

Reflections

How is God calling me (my vocation)?

What must I do to listen to Him?

How do I serve God now?

What is my role in the Church now?

What would God like my role in the Church to be?

How can I know God's will for serving Him
(my mission)?

Describe the state-of-life decisions made by three
people you know.

Prayer

Dear St. Joseph, model of all who are devoted to work and the glory of God, obtain for me the grace to know my talents and abilities and to develop and use them in honor of the Father, Son, and Holy Spirit. I pray that my life may imitate your faithfulness, obedience, and humility. May I seek holiness in all things, especially in the ordinary. I ask this through Christ our Lord. Amen.

Remember

You must seek to know your vocation before being able to respond to it. You must listen for God's call in your life, faithfully following His lead as He guides you in the right choices. If you close your ears to God's call, you are a branch cut off from the true vine—Christ. Then you no longer abide or "rest in Him" but become "independent" in a futile effort to bear fruit.

4
The Branches

The Branches—Your Mission

Discover Your Mission in Life

Sent to carry out God's plan . . . uniquely personal . . . taking many forms.

" . . . lead a life worthy of the calling to which you have been called." (Ephesians 4: 1)

Even if you have yet to discover a state of life, you may still be called to "go forth" and serve Christ in a variety of ways as part of your mission. This can take many forms, all representing smaller branches from the larger limb of the tree. The larger limb represents your vocation; the smaller branches, your mission.

Look at your mission as something much more than career involvement. Your mission is a means of serving an important function within the family of God and being a special part of God's plan.

In His Image

Your mission in life is how God is calling you to serve Him and how you plan to live your life as a reflection of Him.

You are a living portrait of His image in this world. Your mission statement will define how God is calling you to know, love, and serve Him and use the gifts He has given to you.

In General

The great mission for our lives, proclaimed by Jesus Christ Himself, is this:

> "Go therefore and make disciples of all nations, baptizing them in the name of the Father

and of the Son and of the Holy Spirit. . . ." (Matthew 28:19)

We are therefore sent to bear witness to others of Christ.

> You can serve God as a garbage collector, musician, or computer programmer simply by treating others around you with respect and dignity and seeing Christ in them.

Getting Specific

From this general mission to witness to Christ, you can discover how God wants you to work for Him, spreading the gospel message to others. To believe in Christ means to follow His command and the mission found in the passage from St. Matthew above.

Your personal mission begins with this most basic mission mandated by Christ, translated into specific ways in which God leads you to serve Him in daily life. This could be through raising children, promoting fairness in the workplace, helping others less fortunate, participating in parish life, and caring for the elderly, as a few examples. You can serve God as a garbage collector, musician, or computer pro-

grammer simply by treating others around you with respect and dignity and seeing Christ in them. Let the Holy Spirit take over and guide you day by day, week in and week out, year after year. Start each morning by offering the day to God and asking the Holy Spirit to guide you in all of your actions.

You must also take stock of your skills, talents, and abilities (all the gifts that God has given you) and decide how God is calling you to use them. Where does God most want you to apply these gifts, and how can you get there? Consider your area of greatest potential and how you can develop and improve your talents.

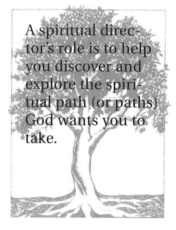

> A spiritual director's role is to help you discover and explore the spiritual path (or paths) God wants you to take.

Getting Help

It is very helpful to have an adult spiritual director guide you as you seek and learn about God's will in your life. This may be a priest, parent, relative, teacher, sister, or brother. Choose someone who has a strong faith and sees God in the activities of daily life.

In receiving spiritual direction, you gain understanding of a particular destination or goal and of the route to follow. In a sense, it is like planning a trip. The path is chosen in accordance with where you want to go. Through discussion, prayer, advice, and other spiritual exercises, a spiritual director can play a major part in helping you discover and understand your purpose in life.

Finding Your Mission

Your mission is a learning experience, not settled once-for-all in a single decision. Rather, your mission becomes more clear in time and may change at different stages of life.

Your mission in life can be expressed in family, school, parish, home, community, work, and leisure activities. You can be a witness to Christ living within you in any of these areas. For example, someone who has a career in management can regularly treat others in a Christlike manner, including other managers, the secretary, the janitor, the waitress at the restaurant—all those who cross his path.

Consider St. Joseph, an example of a witness to God's almighty presence in his life, which greatly overshadows his work as a carpenter.

Similarly, a carpenter who daily works with materials like wood, nails, hammer, and saws can be an image of Christ to fellow carpenters, the construction supervisor, the materials supplier, and in family, neighborhood, and Church contacts.

Remember, it's not so much **what** you do, rather **how** you do it!

In a general sense, it is not so much **what** you do but rather **how** you do it. It is not so much what you accomplish in earthly endeavors but in how Christlike a manner you live your life. Accordingly, your Christian life should be one that uses all the talents and gifts God has provided. Just as you would with a present under the Christmas tree, you're expected to **open** the box, **discover** the contents, then **use** the gift that's inside.

Reflections

MISSION (TO DO WHAT GOD WANTS YOU TO DO)

Answering the following questions may help you discover your mission as God intends.

What is my greatest talent?

How is God calling me to use this talent?

What other person (adult) can help me spiritually discover greater purpose in life?

How can I serve God as a member of His Body— the Church?

In Summary

Vocation is . . .

The UNIVERSAL call

in baptism to live a holy life (this gives life meaning and destiny)

and

The SPECIFIC CHOICE

of a state of life, such as marriage, priesthood, or the consecrated life.

Mission is . . .

The GENERAL WITNESS

to others of Christ in your life

and

LIFEWORK:

The specific use of your God-given abilities to bring glory to God in all you do (for instance, as student, parent, worker).

Your LifeWork is not limited to career or profession but is a personal response to God's call to follow Him and seek Him in all you do, especially with love for others (including those people who bring about difficulty in life).

The choice of a profession or career can be a means of livelihood (monetary gain) and a commitment to use your gifts in a specific way, perhaps as a calling. For example, think of some incredibly gifted musicians who have so much talent; it is hard not to think of their use of these gifts as a calling.

The LifeWork choices can be many and varied and can include career decisions, educational pursuits, recreation and leisure-time activities, and application of your abilities to your vocation and choice of a state in life. Later in this chapter, we will focus on how the career aspect of these LifeWork choices can be explored.

Values and Virtues

What's Valuable?

Values are the worthwhile things we believe in. They have an influence on the majority of our life decisions. These personal values can also have a significant influence on career choices.

A VALUE is something desirable.

WORK VALUES are important qualities in the workplace.

What you value in the workplace and in the rewards of work affects your decisions about many occupational areas. These "work values" can directly affect choices about career goals, employment settings, desire for advancement, and the importance of money.

A VIRTUE is a standard of right or moral excellence, the true north of a moral compass.

Values Involve Choices

A VICE is a moral fault or failing, something that is wrong.

It therefore becomes important to identify the important values in your life in relation to attitudes and feelings toward work. Some examples of work values are the following:

Service to others

(service to individuals, groups, or society in general)

Variety

(change in tasks, duties, surroundings)

Prestige

(respect from others)

Security

Financial reward

Accomplishment

Recognition

Working relationships

Creativity

Leadership

Independence

Artistic expression

Aesthetic expression

Intellectual pursuits

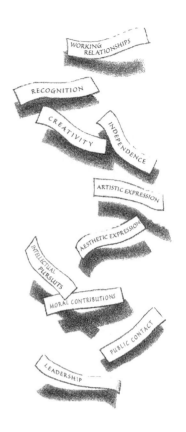

Moral contributions

(work that is relevant to important moral standards)

Public contact

(frequent, daily contact with people)

Many elements of the value system you have come from the influence of parents and family, as well as religious, environmental, cultural, and economic factors. They are the source of many important aspects of our life.

Reflections

Which of the work values on pages 45–47 are most important in your life right now?

1. _____

2. _____

3. _____

Virtues—A Standard for Living

Other factors besides values that influence your life decisions are the personal beliefs you hold about life in general and the amount of virtue or moral goodness that you may (or may not) have.

Virtues are firm attitudes, perfections of mind and will, shining examples of moral excellence, conforming to a Christian standard of the highest good that can be accomplished. Virtues, well practiced, become a habit of choosing excellence in conduct and behavior, based on knowledge of goodness and a standard of **rightness**, merged with integrity of character.

Examples of human virtues are the following:

Compassion

(sensitivity to others' suffering and a desire to help)

Loyalty

(faithfulness)

Honesty

(truth)

Friendship

(companionship)

Courtesy

(accommodation)

Kindness

(generosity, helpfulness)

Fortitude

(courage, boldness, bravery)

Justice

(fairness)

Prudence

(wisdom, insight, understanding)

Temperance

(self-control, restraint, strength of character)

These last four virtues (fortitude, justice, prudence, and temperance) are known as the "cardinal" virtues, from the Latin word for *hinge* since all other virtues, lesser and greater in importance, hinge or pivot on them.

The virtues just described take root in the foundation for Christian moral activity—the three theological virtues:

Faith

> (belief in God and all that He has said and revealed; must be united to hope and charity)

Hope

> (desire for eternal life; relying on the promises of Jesus and grace from the Holy Spirit)

Charity

> (the love of God above all things and our neighbor as ourselves)

Virtues are like a lighthouse that shines its beam through fog. It is a light to follow, even when life's journey is unclear, hazy, or difficult.

Consider the influence of values, virtues, and your faith on the career decision-making process. Discover those elements that are important to you. Then consider what are the most important of these values and virtues in the workplace, particularly qualities such as integrity, punctuality, dependability, acceptance (especially of difficult tasks), and cooperation.

Integrity

> (holding to a moral code)

Punctuality

> (completing tasks early or on time)

Dependability

> (capability of being relied upon)

Acceptance

> (taking responsibility without protest or reaction)

Cooperation

> (working well with others for a common purpose)

It is precisely these traits that make a huge difference in performance levels on the job, differences between an "excellent" worker and an "average" or "satisfactory" worker, between someone well thought of in the workplace and someone "tolerated", and between someone consistently reliable and someone only partially dependable. These qualities, established within the family, usually unfold in the life of a student and tend to reach maturity in the workplace and adulthood.

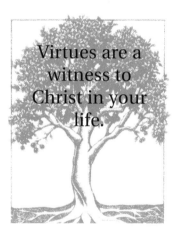

Virtues are a witness to Christ in your life.

what we see as worthwhile or desirable. In essence, we **value** what we **think** is **valuable,** which thus reduces values to thoughts and ideas about things of life. Values can be superficial or misleading, such as our emphasis on fast cars or fashionable clothing. Values can change directions frequently, creating a zig-zag pattern through life.

Values can change direction frequently, creating a zig-zag pattern through one's life.

So What's the Difference?

Values are similar to personal preferences—different for each individual and often changing. We value

Virtues are shining examples of moral excellence—a standard of highest good. They are unchanging qualities of character.

Virtues, unlike values, are unchanging qualities and standards of character that can be taught or acquired in many ways, especially in the home. They are the more significant in maintaining high standards of performance on the job and in other areas of life.

Vices are those habits of thought, word, or deed that are wrong; they are moral faults or failings.

Reflections

What virtues do you possess now?

What virtues would you like to have?

Gifts from God

Our Lord gives many gifts, especially the gift of Himself to **guide,** to **lead,** to **nudge,** to be with you at all times. He is always there. He is present in every situation—the good ones, the bad ones, and the ugly ones. Look at the seven gifts of the Holy Spirit (see Isaiah 11:1–2):

Wisdom

(sound judgment and keen perception; discernment)

Understanding

(insight; awareness; seeing things from the place of another)

Counsel

(advice)

Fortitude

(courage; strength)

Knowledge

(comprehension acquired by experience or study)

Piety

(holy living)

Fear of the Lord

(standing in awe of the Lord; respect)

"To each is given the manifestation of the Spirit for the common good." (1 Corinthians 12:7)

These gifts are freely given by God in the life of the believer, especially in the sacrament of confirmation. In the process of understanding your spiritual gifts, you may also come to a better understanding of the skills and abilities you will use in work and other tasks. The important thing is to be open to what God wants for you.

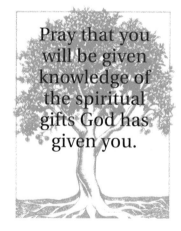

Pray that you will be given knowledge of the spiritual gifts God has given you.

> "Ask, and it will be given you; seek, and you will find; knock, and it will be opened to you. For every one who asks receives, and he who seeks finds, and to him who knocks it will be opened."
> (Matthew 7:7–8)

Doors and Dark Rooms

Picture a door for just a moment, giving special thought to a knob on only **one** side, your side. Christ is on the other side of the door. He has no knob. He always remains there, and His presence is more fully seen as you open the door wider and wider. The dark room becomes filled with light. When you knock, He tells you that the door is unlocked. Turn the knob and it will open. He wants to be Lord of your life— to guide, to lead, to reveal His Father's will for you. However, you need to ask, seek, and knock.

There are other doors. Remember when Joseph and Mary were trying to find lodging for the night in Bethlehem. How many doors remained closed when Joseph knocked on them in his effort to find a birth place for Jesus? How many times since then has Jesus knocked on the door of someone's heart only to have it remain locked from the inside? Unlock your heart and let Jesus fill your life.

St. Elizabeth Ann Seton—
A Protestant Who Became Catholic

U.S. born, Elizabeth married William Seton at the age of nineteen. Their marriage was blessed with great joy, and they had five children. Although wealthy and socially quite active, Elizabeth was devoted to caring for the poor. Her husband eventually lost his fortune and began to fail in health, dying in 1803 after nine years of marriage.

Elizabeth was befriended by a devout Catholic family and joined the Catholic Church in 1805. She opened the first American Catholic school in 1808, and in 1809 she began a community of religious sisters, later called the Daughters of Charity.

January 4

She received the title of "Mother" as head of the community. She also remained a devoted mother to her children and was very loyal to the Church. She died in 1821 and is the first native-born North American to be declared a saint.

She followed God's call to dedicate her life completely to Him. Today, Sisters from the Daughters of Charity carry on Mother Seton's work in schools, hospitals, and homes for the elderly. The importance of God's will was a major part of her spiritual life. She told her Sisters: *"The first end I propose in our daily work is to do the will of God; secondly, to do it in the manner He wills it; and thirdly, to do it because it is His Will."*

Summary

In this first section, we looked more closely at the unique mission God calls each of us to and ways to discover the spiritual gifts, skills, talents, and abilities that we will use in doing His work and living a joyous, fulfilling life. In the next section, we'll focus specifically on the career-planning and decision-making part of the LifeWork process.

Reflections

Is my "door" locked or open to Jesus?

What should I ask of God right now?

How can I seek Him?

Where is He to be found?

How can I be a witness to others of Jesus Christ in my life . . .

    . . . at home?

    . . . at school?

LifeWork Planning and Decision Making

Seeking God's presence in all you do, discover your talents and gifts, gather information, and move in the direction indicated by these elements.

"As each one has received a gift, employ it for one another . . . in order that in everything God may be glorified through Jesus Christ."
(1 Peter 4:10–11)

In choosing a specific career path (such as accountant, teacher, mechanic), you must blend a number of variables together. These variables include the **occupational** elements of:

Talents, skills, and interests

Occupational information

Training and educational options

And the **spiritual** elements of:

Values, virtues, and beliefs

Spiritual gifts

Understanding of God's call in your life

These spiritual elements are illuminated by the light of the Holy Spirit shining through the lens of prayer, Scripture, and Church teaching.

This light helps you become aware of how various spiritual gifts combine with God's call in making important LifeWork decisions.

Coaching

Parents, teachers, guidance specialists, friends, and other adults can help you develop a better understanding of your talents, skills, interests, educational options, and occupational potential.

More about Coaching

It is also very important to find someone who can act as your spiritual guide or coach— directing, leading, encouraging, and being there when you need to talk. Often the coach will be one or both parents. At other times, the coach can be a close friend, family member, priest, religious brother or sister.

As in sports, the coach does not play the game but is there to give feedback and encouragement when you need it.

Can you think of an adult who can fulfill the dual role of career coach and spiritual coach? If so, talk to the person about giving you help in LifeWork planning. Otherwise, seek one adult for career guidance and another for spiritual direction.

Fruit of the Spirit

We must look for the fruits of the Spirit (see pages 89–90) as a means of gauging whether our choices and use of free will are in line with God's plan, especially the fruits of love, joy, and peace. In a sense, we are building a house that has a spiritual foundation and a structure made of occupational elements.

Finding a Balance

One of the greatest challenges in adulthood is to seek a balance between work and other obligations, such as service to others (especially within the Church) and prayer. It is easy to become immersed in a career or hobbies or recreation or travel or sports. It is sometimes hard to integrate things of this world with things of God's world.

"But the fruit of the Spirit is love, joy, peace, patience, kindness, goodness, faithfulness, gentleness, self-control; against such there is no law."
(Galatians 5:22–23)

The choice of a career may be closely interwoven with one's vocation. For example, those who remain **single** may have the greatest number of options for service to others. Thus, the career choice may involve a particularly strong commitment to other people in terms of time and energy.

For **married** people, a balance is very important between career and one's vocation as spouse and parent. Working long, excessive hours in a chosen profession may prove counterproductive to a healthy family life.

"You can't hold two watermelons in one hand." (an old Armenian proverb)

For **priests** and those in the **religious life,** different forms of service may be followed depending on a particular order, congregation, or needs of a diocese. For example, some religious orders have an apostolate of teaching or hospital work or serving the poor. (See "Vocations in the Catholic Church", pp. 109–12.)

"For as in one body we have many members, and all the members do not have the same function, so we, though many, are one body in Christ, and individually members one of another. Having gifts that differ according to the grace given to us, let us use them. . . ."
(Romans 12:4–6)

Talents and Skills

Everyone has different **talents** and **abilities,** things they are good at doing and which can be developed to the fullest possible extent. These talents are often transformed into skills that are used in a chosen profession or career and other parts of one's life.

Talents are natural abilities or acquired skills.

Your talents can take you in many directions. You may be interested in a particular type of career or job, hobbies, recreation, types of people or organizations, and leisure-time pursuits.

Skills are the ability to do something competently and well.

A **skill** is the ability to do something well. Your strongest skills can be developed and improved. You have many skills, including those that relate to work, called **job-related skills**. Other skills may relate to school subjects, called **academic skills**. Special skills related to performance of a particular job are called **occupational skills**. Finally, skills that can be applied to different types of jobs are called **transferable skills**. You may have a variety of other abilities, too, such as communication, organizational, managerial, and public-contact skills.

Reflections

What are your skills now?

Job-Related Skills:

Academic Skills:

What skills would you like to have?

Job-Related Skills:

Academic Skills:

Interests

Interests about work and careers may initially stem from activities and school subjects that bring a sense of satisfaction. Job satisfaction creates a situation where work is more than just a way to earn a living.

Interests are the focus of your attention, concern, or curiosity.

Career **interests** can be evaluated using the following three approaches:

....

1. Data—People—Things

2. Occupational Groups

3. Career Clusters

_____

1. Data—People—Things

Most jobs require you to function in some way with data, people, or things. Interests (and skills) can be placed into one or a combination of these three groups.

Data

Working with information, knowledge, and concepts related to data, people, or things using observation, investigation, interpretation, visualization, and mental creation. Also includes creating and developing ideas, gathering facts, and working with numbers, words, and symbols.

JOB EXAMPLES
Accountant, Artist, Laboratory Technician, Research Engineer, Computer Programmer

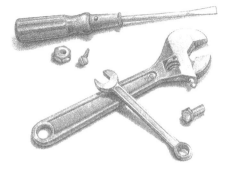

People

Working with individuals or groups of people; includes animals dealt with on an individual basis. Skills and abilities include persuading, supervising, instructing, counseling, helping, and serving.

JOB EXAMPLES

Teacher, Guidance Specialist, Attorney, Veterinarian, Nurse, Salesperson

Things

Working with tools, equipment, machinery, and products—objects, substances, or materials that are not living. Includes doing precision work, operating or controlling equipment, driving, and handling items.

JOB EXAMPLES

Machinist, Electronics Technician, Mechanic, Truck Driver, Assembler

Reflections

Think for a moment about your interest in *Data, People,* and *Things*. Place these three categories in order of your preference.

1. _____

2. _____

3. _____

Do the skills you listed on pages 62–63 relate to your *First Choice* on page 64? For example, if your first choice is *People,* do you have skills in listening, speaking, and helping others?

State your *First Choice* of Interests:

(*from your list on page 64*)

(Data, People, or Things)

What are your *Related Skills:*

(*from your list on pages 62–63*)

(Related Skills)

What occupations might relate to your first choice of interests?

1. _____

2. _____

3. _____

What leisure-time activities relate to your first choice of interests?

1. _____

2. _____

3. _____

2. Occupational Groups

A second approach to career interests is the use of occupational categories. *The Dictionary of Occupational Titles* (U.S. Department of Labor, 1991, revised 4th edition) lists the following nine general categories of occupations:

....

Professional, Technical, and Managerial

Clerical and Sales

Service

Agricultural, Fishery, Forestry

Processing

Machine Trades

Benchwork

Miscellaneous (including transportation, packaging, entertainment, and graphic arts)

More specific occupational categories can then be placed under these general headings.

Professional, Technical, and Managerial

Architecture, engineering, and surveying
Mathematics and physical sciences
Computer-related occupations
Life sciences
Social sciences
Medicine and health
Education
Museum, library, and archival sciences
Law and jurisprudence
Religion and theology
Writing
Art
Entertainment and recreation
Administrative specializations
Managers and officials

Clerical and Sales

Stenography, typing, filing, etc.
Computing and account-recording
Production and stock clerks
Information and message distribution
Miscellaneous clerical
Sales—Service, consumable commodities, or commodities

Service

Domestic service
Food and beverage preparation and service
Lodging and related service
Barbering, cosmetology, and related service
Amusement and recreation service
Miscellaneous personal service
Apparel and furnishings service
Protective service
Building and related service

Agricultural, Fishery, Forestry

Plant farming
Animal farming
Fishery
Forestry
Hunting, trapping

Processing

Processing metal
Ore refining and foundry work

Processing food, tobacco, and related products

Processing paper and related materials

Processing petroleum, coal, natural and manufactured gas, and related products

Processing chemicals, plastics, synthetics, rubber, paint, and related products

Processing wood and wood products

Processing stone, clay, glass, and related products

Processing leather, textiles, and related products

Machine Trades

Metal machining

Metalworking

Mechanics and machinery repairs

Paperworking

Printing

Wood machining

Machining stone, clay, glass, and related materials

Textiles

Machine trades

Benchwork

Fabrication, assembly, and repair of metal products

Fabrication and repair of scientific, medical, photographic, optical, horological, and related products

Assembly and repair of electrical equipment

Fabrication and repair of products made from assorted materials

Painting, decorating, and related services

Fabrication and repair of plastics, synthetics, rubber, and related products

Fabrication and repair of wood products

Fabrication and repair of sand, stone, clay, and glass products

Fabrication and repair of textile, leather, and related products

Structural Work

Metal fabricating

Welding, cutting, and related work

Electrical assembling, installing, and repairing

Painting, plastering, waterproofing, cementing, and related work

Excavating, grading, paving, and related work

Construction

Structural work

Miscellaneous

Motor freight

Transportation

Packaging and materials handling

Extraction of minerals

Production and distribution of utilities

Amusement, recreation, motion picture, radio, and television

Graphic arts

Reflections

From these occupational groups, choose the top five (in order of preference, if possible) and the bottom five (least desirable).

My "top five" occupational groups:

1. _____

2. _____

3. _____

4. _____

5. _____

My "bottom five" occupational groups:

1. _____

2. _____

3. _____

4. _____

5. _____

3. Career Clusters

Finally, the third approach to understanding your career interests and a way to apply talents and skills is to place similar occupations in groups called *Clusters*.

The following list of career clusters (from *The Guide for Occupational Exploration*) includes descriptions that illustrate the kind of work people do and how your abilities might fit.

....

Artistic
> An interest in the creative expression of feelings or ideas.

Scientific
> An interest in discovering, collecting, and analyzing information about the natural world and in ap-

plying scientific research findings to problems in medicine, the life sciences, and the natural sciences.

Plants and Animals

An interest in working with plants and animals, usually in an outdoor setting.

Protective

An interest in using authority to protect people and property.

Mechanical

An interest in applying mechanical principles to practical situations by use of machines or hand tools.

Industrial

An interest in repetitive, concrete, organized activities often done in a factory setting.

Business Detail

An interest in organized, clearly defined activities requiring accuracy and attention to details, primarily in an office setting.

Selling

An interest in bringing others to a particular point of view by personal persuasion, using sales and promotional techniques.

Accommodating

An interest in catering to the wishes and needs of others, usually on a one-to-one basis.

Humanitarian

An interest in helping others with their mental, spiritual, social, physical, or vocational needs.

Leading and Influencing

An interest in leading and influencing others by using high-level verbal or numerical abilities.

Physical Performing

An interest in physical activities performed before an audience.

Reflections

As before, from these career clusters, choose the top five (in order of preference, if possible) and the bottom five (least desirable).

My "top five" career clusters:

1. _____

2. _____

3. _____

4. _____

5. _____

My "bottom five" career clusters:

1. _____

2. _____

3. _____

4. _____

5. _____

How well do these choices match with your selections in Data-People-Things and the Occupational Groups?

Clusters can also be related to school subjects, such as chemistry, biology, and physics for the scientific cluster, and computer operation, typing, and bookkeeping for business details. Which school subjects are relevant to your career clusters?

Other Approaches to Learning More about Talents, Skills, and Interests

There are a variety of other approaches to learning more about your talents, skills, and interests. These include identifying your "likes" and "dislikes" (or "favorite" and "least favorite") in a number of areas such as those listed below.

	Favorite	Least Favorite
Hobbies, leisure time, recreational pursuits		
Books and magazines		
Kinds of people		
Places		
School subjects		

Gathering Information

The choices made in identifying your talents, skills, and interests are the first steps in deciding where you might begin to gather more information. The types of information that can be helpful in establishing a career goal include **measuring** your skills, interests, and abilities, obtaining detailed **job information** (such as descriptions of jobs and labor market trends), and identifying **training and educational resources**.

Assessment

Measuring your skills, interests, and abilities is called assessment. Important skills to measure include **academic abilities** (especially reading, spelling, mathematical, and language skills), coupled with your **aptitude** (potential) for types of tasks, along with **interest** level and motivation for a specific career path.

School performance and achievement testing can be very useful in measuring your strengths and weaknesses. Vocational testing can be helpful in defining abilities in the academic areas as well as aptitudes (for example, clerical, mechanical, and technical skills and dexterity), and general interests. Career guidance centers in the school setting or private career counselors can be used for assessment. **Test scores, however, are only indicators and not the last word on your potential; they do not necessarily indicate**

what God may be calling you to do.

Steer clear of the myth that a job that pays well will make you happy.

Occupational Information

The Labor Market

Another step in career planning involves gaining knowledge about the job market, especially learning whether or not certain occupations are in demand. In other words, can you get a job when you have completed your education? What is the demand for a particular job? Starting salary? Advancement potential? Training and educational requirements? Certification or licensure requirements? It is important to gather information about the labor market, especially as you embark on an educational journey leading toward a specific career.

Labor market information can be obtained from a variety of sources, including the following:

1. School guidance/career planning centers
2. State employment services

3. Trade and professional organizations
4. Private or adult school placement offices
5. Newspapers
6. U.S. Department of Labor, Bureau of Labor Statistics
7. Information gathered personally from others by "informational interviewing"
8. Volunteer work

The mountain leading toward a difficult-to-find job is often steep but not impossible to climb. Labor market knowledge helps you gain as much information as possible regarding what to look for before you begin the climb. Good decisions are based on good information and, of course, prayer.

Even if your choice is not one justified by the current demands of the labor market, the knowledge of potential difficulties in finding work becomes valuable in planning a job search strategy when you complete school.

You should also keep in mind that the data about job openings can sometimes be a bit dated, sometimes several months old or longer. Your career decisions may involve a period of time for education, causing the labor market information to be even more outdated.

Strong Interests and Motivation

Employment trends may be a lot different when you complete training and start a job search. It is more important to consider your interests, skills, abilities, and motivation for a chosen career. Remember, your talents can be used to fill a job opening, even if there is a downward trend in the labor market for a specific career. Persistent effort often wins out on the path toward finding work, even if few openings exist.

Many openings will be available as a result of growth (new jobs) and replacements. For example, from 1992 to 2005 there will be a 32 percent increase in accountants and auditors in the United States, or 304,000 new positions, plus additional openings due to separations from employment.

Most of the time, areas of strong interest and motivation can be turned into employment, even though "trends" in the labor market may be negative rather than positive.

Employment "Trends"

Many career seekers often place an emphasis on the jobs and industries that promise employment due to strong growth, but this may lead to an unwise career choice, incompatible with interests, talents, and calling. Growth factors can change, especially by the time you finish your education.

Reflections

Make some initial efforts to acquire information about a job that interests you.

First, identify an occupation that has some interests to you and about which you would like to obtain more information:

Occupational Title _____

Choose two approaches or sources of gaining information about this occupation and list them below. Use the list of sources on pages 72–73.

1. _____

2. _____

Plan to obtain the desired information within thirty days. The process of gathering information also helps to check the "fit of the garment", like trying on clothes for size and appearance, to determine if you are on the right career track.

A Fork in the Road

It is also important to know **why** a particular career or job seems interesting, especially if there are shifts in the labor market requiring a change in employment situations. You can still be heading in the right direction consistent with your sense of **mission**, even if the world of employment has unexpected changes. You may be faced with a decision, like a fork in the road, that requires involvement in a different type of job but with your overall mission preserved. You would still use the talents and skills God has given to you.

Education and Training Options

There are many approaches to gaining skills and training for a chosen occupation.

High School

Some skills for employment can be learned in a high school offering vocational classes for positions such as secretary, bookkeeper, and food service worker.

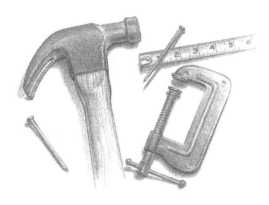

Apprenticeship

Skills can be gained through a formal program of on-the-job training and classroom instruction. An apprentice learns a trade from experienced workers, assisting them in real job situations and working under their supervision. Apprenticeships are sponsored jointly by unions and employers. The program may last from one to six years before one is fully qualified or at the journeyman level within a specific trade.

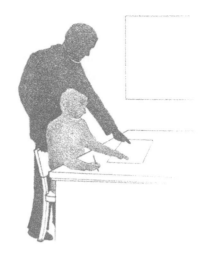

On-the-Job Training

Skills can be learned from more experienced workers in a less formal way than through an apprenticeship. Some classroom instruction may also be involved. The length of time for on-the-job training varies widely depending on the occupation—sometimes one or two days, other times a year or longer. Acquired job skills come about by watching and helping other workers and performing job tasks under supervision.

Military Training

Job skills and work experience can be gained while in the military service. Such training can involve a combination of direct work experience and/or classroom instruction. Skills that are acquired can often be used in civilian employment.

Vocational Education

This type of training can involve adult schools, private business colleges, technical institutes, trade schools, and home study courses. The typical emphasis is on specific skills needed to do the job. Some trade schools are accredited for earning college units, but many do not offer college units, and completion results in a certificate rather than a degree. Many vocational and technical school programs also provide job placement assistance.

Community and Junior Colleges

Specific job skills can be acquired often within one year by pursuing a certificate of achievement program, with an emphasis on those skills needed for the job, but usually without taking general educa-

tion course work (i.e., history, biology, English). Other programs involve acquiring an associate degree within a two-year period of time with an emphasis on job skills but coupled with a broader education than the certificate program. Transfer programs are also available in many community and junior colleges, allowing one to prepare to enter a college or university offering a bachelor's degree. Transfer programs usually last two years.

Colleges and Universities

A bachelor's degree is typically earned with a major (specialty area) in at least one specific subject. Most bachelor's degree programs last four to five years and can be followed by graduate or professional study leading toward a master's degree (usually one to two years), and/or a Ph.D. (usually two years or longer), or a professional degree in areas like medicine, law, and pharmacy. An undergraduate program (bachelor's degree) provides skills that can usually apply to many different types of occupations, not just one specific job.

Reflections

Select your preference for learning job skills based on the training and education categories described on pages 75–76.

My education preference is:

Length of time I can commit to training:

Consider some ways that you can obtain information about training resources.

☐ Visit a school or schools and speak to staff members about specific programs.

☐ Obtain catalogues or brochures from schools.

What can you do now to gain more information about a school or training program?

Once I get the information, I will discuss it with:

Think of a parent or other important adult who can help you as a "LifeWork Coach", someone who can provide encouragement, support, and advice when you need it.

Building the House

You have looked at talents, skills, and interests and considered the job market and training options. The process of putting all these factors together can be illustrated by the various stages of home construction.

In the design stage, drawings are made of the house and structure. These plans eventually will become the final blueprint. In the process of working out the details of your "career design", you evaluate interests, skills, abilities, and related information in selecting a career goal.

Next is the preparation stage (the details and working plan), followed by construction. For the career-minded, this means establishing a goal and then taking the steps to achieve it.

The choice of career (or at least a career cluster) should occur before the plans are drawn up or at some early stage in the planning.

Pray daily for the hand of God, the Master Carpenter, to guide you as you build your "house".

Board by board the walls take shape, and eventually a house is built—the house becomes a home. Just as the home can be changed or remodeled, so, too, a career develops and unfolds.

Identify the value you have placed on money and your expectations for wages or salary. Although money can be an important part of the decision-making process, you must decide its priority in relation to other parts of your life, such as the spiritual aspects, your values and beliefs. Money can be viewed as a by-product of work, or it can be elevated to an unhealthy level above all things so that work and the expected monetary outcome take precedence over other important parts of life (such as family).

Consider this: Running a home can also be a career choice! It involves a combination of talents, skills, and interests and is a chosen path for many who elect to use their abilities elsewhere than in the formal labor market.

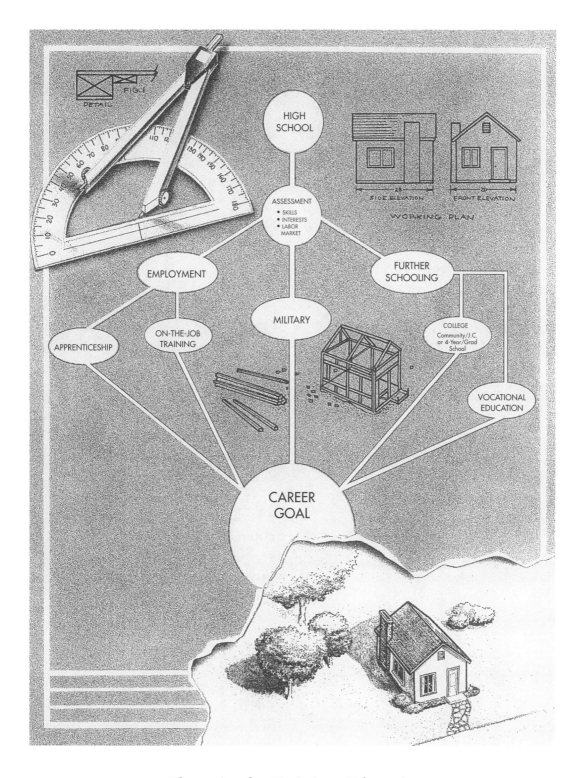

Blueprint for Training, Education,
and Career Choices

Putting the Pieces Together

Making LifeWork decisions is like putting a puzzle together. The puzzle on the next page represents those elements that shape and define your choices in life—your LifeWork choices. The pieces, when put together properly, make a beautiful picture of your response to God in **all** aspects of life, especially in the many activities and pursuits that portray your mission. The picture in the puzzle is a portrait of you, of how you live your life while using the gifts God has given to you. This is your faith put into action as an ambassador of Christ.

You may not be able to describe each puzzle piece, yet knowing about some of the pieces offers a glimpse of the finished picture. That is exactly why you can serve God at all times in your life, whether you have much knowledge about yourself or only a little knowledge. The key is to focus on the source of all light—God Almighty.

Look at the illustration on page 81, then complete the puzzle piece themes on the next two pages (as many as possible). The completed Puzzle is a composite of yourself and your LifeWork choices, including choice of profession or career, ways of serving the Church, helping the less fortunate, and growing in faith.

LifeWork Choices

The completed puzzle forms an image of your LifeWork choices. Even a partially completed puzzle provides a sense of direction and mission.

LifeWork

TALENTS AND SKILLS

_____
_____
_____
_____
_____
_____
_____
_____

VIRTUES

_____
_____
_____
_____
_____
_____
_____
_____

INTERESTS

_____
_____
_____
_____
_____
_____
_____
_____

WORK VALUES

_____
_____
_____
_____
_____
_____
_____
_____

EDUCATION

_____
_____
_____
_____
_____

_____
_____
_____
_____
_____

GOD'S CALL
(to holiness and
a state of life)

**OCCUPATIONAL
INFORMATION**

_____
_____
_____
_____
_____
_____
_____

_____
_____
_____
_____
_____

GENERAL MISSION
(witness to Christ)

**SPIRITUAL
DIRECTION**

_____
_____
_____
_____
_____
_____
_____
_____
_____
_____

Summary

Your personal mission—your personal way of following Jesus.

Your personal mission is a unique part of the Church's mission—your personal way of following Jesus. Although you will typically establish goals along the way (such as a college major or occupational decisions), it is far more important to have a broader commitment to follow Christ in all parts of your life. You can view your skills, aptitudes, abilities, and other talents as gifts from the Father, gifts to be developed and used during the time you have on earth. Failure to use these gifts narrows your response to God's call.

Your skills, abilities, and talents are gifts from God, gifts to be developed and used.

You must also be careful to avoid activities that bear no real fruit and are essentially useless in the overall view of personal mission. This often includes overindulgence in things of this world, such as excessive involvement in television viewing, hobbies, recreation, music, computers, sports, and other forms of passive entertainment. It is important to keep a balance between these worldly interests and those that relate directly to serving God. By serving God first, others second, and yourself third, you will be well on the way to a life of charity and joy.

Like a compass that points north, our lives are pointed in baptism to God. We hope that we will remain pointed in that direction throughout our life.

The process of making important LifeWork choices involves gathering information about yourself, seeking the guidance of the Holy Spirit, and then gradually narrowing choices down to a realistic goal, all within a setting of prayer.

For example, in career decision making, there is some built-in difficulty for many young people because there are so many occupational categories to choose from. Part of the process of choosing a career involves gaining information about various areas that might be of interest. You can then begin the process of elimination, choosing those that fit better than others and eventually moving toward an occupational group or career cluster that is the best fit, then "fine-tuning" to arrive at a specific career choice.

In seeking God's will for your personal vocation, mission, and LifeWork choices, prayer and guidance from a spiritual director will add much to having a clear view of His plan for your life and your purpose in serving God.

Reflections

What can I eliminate from my life right now that does not contribute to my personal vocation and mission, my personal way of following Jesus?

What gifts has God given to me that need to be developed and used?

Consider keeping a LifeWork journal with weekly entries on matters related to personal vocation and mission. Thoughts about your state of life, God's will for you, concerns about work and career, and your prayer life can be written in your journal.

Prayer

Lord, I thank You for the gifts You have given me, especially for life, love, family, and friends. Help me to know myself better and to know my talents, as I pray, study, and decide on my life's work.

Help me to see and understand the path You open for me. Help me to choose a life's work that will be in response to my potential and Your will for me.

Give me a generous heart to respond to Your challenging call and the strength to follow You wherever You lead me. May I discover Your gentle Presence in choosing a state of life, such as marriage, the priesthood, or consecrated life. Amen.

Remember

The best way to establish a solid career choice is to seek God's will and presence in all you do, understand the talents and skills He has given to you, gather information about careers and the labor market, then move in the direction indicated by these signs and your interests.

5

The Fruit

The Fruit—
Harvest Time

A season to gather a ripened, developed crop, the result of careful, focused, and diligent cultivation. The outcome: our unique way to follow Jesus Christ.

"And I am sure that he who began a good work in you will bring it to completion at the day of Jesus Christ." (Philippians 1:6)

Probably the best way of knowing whether you are living out your mission in accordance with God's will is to look for the fruits. The fruits of the Holy Spirit are love, joy, peace, patience, kindness, goodness, faithfulness, gentleness, self-control, generosity, modesty, and chastity.

To be fruitful means to grow in grace, filling our lives with Jesus and the fullness of the Holy Spirit. Look over the fruits of the Spirit shown here. Which ones are present in your life? Which ones have yet to be produced in you?

Love

(love patterned after God's love for you)

Joy

(great pleasure and delight)

Peace

(an inward quality that brings with it serenity of mind)

Patience

(endurance—bearing up under the stresses and strains of life)

Kindness

(a tender, considerate, and helping nature)

Goodness

(manifestation of an upright, thoughtful, loyal, obedient nature)

Faithfulness

(reliability, dependability, and responsibility in dealing with others)

Gentleness

(willingness to submit to the will of God)

Self-Control

(mastery over feelings, desires, and actions)

Generosity

(willingness to give of yourself and your possessions)

Modesty

(humble and moderate estimate of your value, abilities, and achievements; unpretentiousness and dignity in manner and conduct)

Chastity

(sexual purity; simplicity of style)

Branching Out

As you move along in your work, you as a "little branch" must remember that God may have new and different ways to use you in

"The fruit of the righteous is a tree of life. . . ." (*Proverbs 11:30*)

this life. Other small branches may spring forth, such as ministries within the Church or new ways of using your talents. These branches become an essential part of your mission, of being sent, of following Jesus.

It would be easy to see yourself as simply a limb (for example, marriage and family) with a single small branch extending from it (career). How much more may our Lord have in store for you? That is precisely why you need to **pray, pray, pray** . . . to remain in the ongoing presence of the Father, always approaching Him as a child.

Pray daily!

Gift Growers

You also need to think about the many abilities and gifts you have been given, perhaps identified in part through this book. With these abilities and gifts . . .

> *nourish* them . . .
>
> *practice* them . . .
>
> *expand* them . . .
>
> *grow* them . . .
>
> *use* them . . .

. . . to the fullest extent possible, **all to God's glory.**

Be Careful!!

A word of caution: Try to be oriented toward the **root** and not the **fruit,** growing in grace and holiness while remaining or abiding in Him. Fruit will be born in accord with the Holy Spirit, flowing through the tree into the limbs and branches. This will produce a special sense of joy, peace, and contentment. The experience of joy is often much deeper and real than the passing pleasures of this life (such as a good meal) or happiness (based on something "happening").

Reflections

Consider family members and friends who you believe have entered life and work situations filled with God's peace and joy. Who are they?

Discuss with them how they arrived at various major life decisions.

Identify people who serve as examples of living a faith-filled life—past and present. After each name, identify qualities in them that appeal to you.

Name   Qualities that appeal to you

_____   _____

_____   _____

_____   _____

_____   _____

_____   _____

Changing Direction

As you move forward in your mission, it might be necessary to make adjustments along the way, such as in an evolving career (for example, from nurse's aide to licensed vocational nurse to registered nurse; from bookkeeper to certified public accountant). You may also need to change careers, making dramatic shifts in what you do for a living. Keep in mind the building process you have established, founded on prayer and the spiritual life, combined with information gathering and assessment. It is the spiritual food that sustains you during "construction" and follows you along the journey regardless of twists, turns, and forks in the road, assuring you that you are rooted in faith and nourished by God's grace.

"A sound tree cannot bear evil fruit, nor can a bad tree bear good fruit." (Matthew 7:18)

". . . every branch that does bear fruit he prunes, that it may bear more fruit." (John 15:2)

Pruning the Branches

In the powerful yet simple parable of the vine and branches, even branches bearing fruit are pruned. This is why sometimes a change of direction becomes necessary even when life and work appear to be going well. Suppose someone is perfectly content in their present circumstances: good marriage, stable job, wide circle of friends, financial security, and parish activities. Then a new challenge arises within the parish requiring a commitment to take on something new (such as teaching a confirmation class). This may necessitate a great deal of preparation and a reminder that additional fruit will be born of such efforts, but only in time, as the class progresses.

Consider this:

Start a journal or diary that records your walk with Jesus and your efforts to hear His call and respond faithfully.

We are blessed with a personal God who continues to reveal Himself throughout life. Once God's will is known and accepted, our commitments and decisions, (for example, job choices) need to be fulfilled in a manner faithful to God's call. This will likely require us to make further decisions along the way, all the while keeping the focus on our Father, avoiding distractions and detours.

"And whatever you do, in word or deed, do everything in the name of the Lord Jesus, giving thanks to God the Father through him."
(Colossians 3:17)

Continuing Education

Regardless of your chosen work, you can grow in faith by prayer, sacraments, and other forms of devotion, and especially by Scripture reading. Find good books that explain the Catholic faith and help you understand why you believe what you believe (see resources at the end of this book). Be able to answer questions that may come up about topics not easily understood by non-Catholic Christians, as well as non-Christians, like the role of Mary in our Faith, the origin of the sacraments, the Pope, praying for the dead, and the Real Presence of Christ in the Eucharist.

Continue glorifying God by doing well in your work. Try to do the best you possibly can at whatever you pursue, all to God's glory.

Do your best . . .
God will do the rest.

Retirement and Beyond

At some point in life, you will probably retire from the world of work. Remember the tree. Even with retirement, the small branches may take on new appearances and continue to bear much fruit, nourished by the roots that are firmly planted in the soil of faith. Seek the Lord's guidance as you eventually approach retirement. Use your fruit to feed those who are poor, not just economically poor, but those who suffer from spiritual poverty as well.

In the end, your life will be remembered not so much by the career you chose or how much money you made but by your personal qualities and your ability to be like a vital, fruit-bearing tree, firmly rooted in a strong faith.

"You did not choose me, but I chose you and appointed you that you should go and bear fruit. . . ."
(John 15:16)

St. Thomas More—The Lawyer Saint

Thomas More planned to be a priest but decided to study law and entered the English Parliament in 1504. He married and had four children. He led his family in prayer and Scripture reading, and when his wife died, he married a widow for the sake of the children. He became Chancellor of England, a position second only to the King. He refused to approve the divorce asked by King Henry VIII and refused to sign a document acknowledging the King as head of the Catholic Church in England. He resigned from his position as Chancellor and was eventually imprisoned for over a year, suffering greatly in the dungeon known as the "Tower of London". During that time, he wrote to his daughter: *"I trust only in God's merciful goodness. His grace has strengthened me till now and made me content to lose goods, land, and life as well, rather than swear against my conscience. I will not mistrust him. . . ."* In his final words before his execution in 1535, he said that he was *"the King's good servant, but God's first."*

June 22

Thomas gives an example of following God's will throughout his life, holding steadfast to Jesus' call to "Follow Me." He lived his personal vocation and mission as devoted husband and father, lawyer, Chancellor, and a man of faith and strong moral principles.

Summary

Bearing fruit is often the most visible sign of God's presence in your life. Although changes and adjustments may be made along the way of life, you can seek God in all things, including work, leisure, and eventually retirement.

God calls you to follow Him throughout life, even into your retirement, into widowhood, into disabling conditions, sickness, and other circumstances you may face along the way. Ultimately, you will follow Him into death.

Reflections

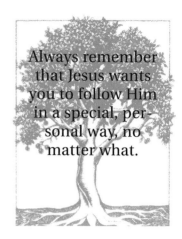

Always remember that Jesus wants you to follow Him in a special, personal way, no matter what.

Identify ways you may hear God's call:

Identify three people who can help you hear and understand God's call:

      1.

      2.

      3.

Identify and list three distractions in your life that might interfere with hearing God's call:

      1.

      2.

      3.

How can you better listen for God's call in your life right now?

How can you bring Jesus to others in your life right now?

What lifelong commitment are you called to in bringing Jesus to others?

You can bring Jesus to others in some way, no matter how small—and you can do this in whatever situation currently occupies your time, such as school, work, home, play, or parish activity. You can do this right now in whatever situation you find yourself, whether you are in high school, college, or an adult in midlife.

Prayer

Eternal God and Father, all glory and honor and praise be Yours. As St. Joseph was completely surrendered to Your will and divine presence, may I also approach You with humility and obedience, seeking the grace to know the state of life that Your Providence has chosen for me and to grow steadily with increasing knowledge of Your will. As it unfolds throughout my life, I pray that I may follow Your will faithfully. I also pray that I will hear Your call throughout my life and always respond with a loving and generous, "Yes." Lord, may Your will be done, and may I always remain Your loving, faithful servant through Christ our Lord. Amen.

Remember

Be ready to make adjustments along the way, especially if it becomes obvious that a decision has not born fruit.

Parents' Guide

Seed to Harvest— Parents' Guide

Every child is uniquely gifted by God. Parenting is an adventure with the aim to help young people become all God has designed them to be, to discover their gifts and to encourage their development.

"Train up a child in the way he should go, and when he is old he will not depart from it."
(Proverbs 22:6)

Pope John Paul II in his 1994 *Letter to Families*, states:

"Parents are the first and most important educators of their own children, and they also possess a fundamental competence in this area: they are educators because they are parents . . . and . . . within the context of education, due attention must be paid to the essential question of **choosing a vocation**, and . . . in particular that of preparing for marriage."

He also describes the family as a "domestic church".

In order to foster wise and prayerful vocational choices, parents must encourage their children to seek *God's call.*

for parents . . .

Encourage your children

to **listen and see** how God is working in their lives, to look for signs and indicators of His will and His presence.

Pray with your children

and encourage them to seek God in private, daily prayer and in communal prayer at Mass.

Talk regularly to your children

about how God seems to be present in their lives and in your life.

Tell about your vocation

and choices you have made along the way in seeking to follow Jesus.

With regard to choosing a career,

encourage your children to gather information about their interests by talking with others and also by acquiring printed material.

Help your children

discover their God-given talents and skills.

Offer examples

from the lives of other family members, past and present, about vocation, mission, and faith decisions.

Allow your children

to blossom at their pace (not your pace).

Remind your children

(and yourself) that adjustments are often required to stay on course.

". . . having the eyes of your hearts enlightened, that you may know what is the hope to which he has called you, what are the riches of his glorious inheritance in the saints, and what is the immeasurable greatness of his power in us who believe, according to the working of his great might."
(Ephesians 1:18–19)

Let's Be Specific . . . What Families Can Do

Here are twenty separate activities that families can use to foster and encourage important LifeWork decisions in their children. Be creative in coming up with other ideas and approaches that will enhance your children's awareness of God's call and their response.

1. Develop a **family tree** of LifeWork choices showing the different vocations and/or careers held by relatives, past and present.

2. Write a **family mission statement** with the participation of all family members. Describe what the purpose of your family should be.

3. As a family, pray for Church vocations and the grace for your children to discern their vocation and God's will.

4. Invite a priest, religious brother, or sister for dinner with your family.

5. Encourage your children's involvement in parish activities.

6. Have your children read a story about a particular saint and discuss their impressions with you.

7. Present the various virtues that are important in your life (including those that are a struggle), and learn about the virtues that are meaningful to your children.

8. Pray together that all LifeWork choices will be in line with God's will. Pray a rosary together for this intention.

9. Talk with your children about how they view their greatest strengths and weaknesses and how their best abilities can be translated into serving God in the working world.

10. Keep momentum going with your children, especially during the high-school years, by regular chats about their response to God and the discovery of their personal vocation.

11. Discuss jobs in the surrounding community that provide service to the family unit, then explore

ways your children can be of service to others.

12. Discuss the reasons people work, and have your children explain how they view the working world. Include discussion about nonpaid careers, such as those of homemaker and of people who volunteer for the service of others.

13. Arrange for your son or daughter to be involved in volunteer work within the community, such as in hospitals, homeless shelters, outreach programs, and nursing homes.

14. Discuss some of the life decisions you made, from high school to the present. Include decisions about your vocation, education, work, and personal interests.

15. Have your children describe their best school subjects and relate them to various jobs or career clusters. Alternately, discuss one of your children's interests, hobbies, recreational, or leisure-time pursuits and relate it to possible careers or jobs.

16. Arrange for your children to "shadow" someone in his workplace, spending two to four hours in job shadowing. Discuss their impressions (such as likes, dislikes, interesting observations).

17. Go with your children to a college, university, vocational school, or other training facility for experience in gathering program information firsthand.

18. Discuss activities than can begin upon high-school completion for the uncertain, undecided, or confused (such as taking general education coursework, exploratory courses in potential interest areas, or employment/on-the-job experience).

19. As your children progress through high school and the early college years, have at least monthly talks (at a "special place", if possible) to review their ongoing thoughts about vocation, mission, God's call, and related LifeWork choices.

20. Adore Jesus together in the presence of the Eucharist or in front of the tabernacle.

Your Most Important Role!

Your most important role is to listen and gently guide your child.

Encourage

Prayer . . .

Discussion . . .

Scripture reading . . .

Regular Mass attendance . . .

Exploration and research . . .

Encourage visitation of

Schools . . .

Employment settings . . .

People in particular occupations . . .

Greatly encourage involvement in parish life.

Avoid

Selling . . .

Preaching . . .

Persuading . . .

Do not engage in

Battles . . .

Confrontation . . .

Value judgments . . .

Making decisions for your children . . .

Encourage talking with others to gather information.

Career Guidance

During the career decision-making aspects of this book, you should work with your children gradually to narrow the choices to a single goal, or at least to a small number of potential goals or career clusters. Once this occurs, your children can then begin exploring careers in an effort to choose occupational goals that are consistent with their interests, talents, and gifts. Remember, there is **not just one right job** for each one but a **number of choices** that would probably work well. Focus more on having a well-thought-out career choice or profession that is aligned with the mission they have discovered.

Prayer

Dear Lord, guide me as the parent of this child as decisions are formed about vocation, mission, and other important parts of life. Help me provide the right words of encouragement, support, and advice. Make me an instrument of Your will so that my child can discover meaning and purpose in life and make wise choices in accordance with Your divine plan. Amen.

Remember

Parenting is an adventure. It is the parents' privilege and responsibility to help their children discover their vocation and mission in life and to develop their talents, gifts, and abilities to be used for the glory of God.

Vocations in the Catholic Church

Vocations in the Catholic Church

Called to be holy, called to serve Him in a particular state of life, chosen according to God's purpose for a vocation and for a specific mission.

"For God's gifts and his call are irrevocable."
(Romans 11:29)

There are many choices one faces in the world of work, particularly in selecting a career (13,000 different job categories!). However, there are only a handful of choices for those seeking God's will for a specific vocation.

Following are brief summaries of the common vocations to which one is called. Also included are some of the typical occupations that can be found in the Catholic Church, along with volunteer activities that can be pursued. The list does not contain all the possibilities that exist. God is full of surprises and may reveal a path that was not expected or considered.

With a commitment to regular, daily prayer, ask God to reveal His will for your vocation and to guide you in choosing activities that make up your LifeWork.

"The harvest is plentiful, but the laborers are few; pray therefore the Lord of the harvest to send out laborers into his harvest."
(Matthew 9:37b–38)

Vocations

Religious life is a call to live a full and satisfying life, serving Jesus and making the gospel message visible to others. A calling to the priesthood or religious life is a unique vocation in the Catholic Church, involving a permanent commitment to serving God and others. Pray that God will reveal His will in your life and that you will respond generously.

Diocesan Priest

Man of faith and prayer serving the people of God in a specific community or diocese, often in a parish, but also in administration or ministries in hospital, prison, or campus settings. Promises chastity and obedience to the bishop. Minister of the sacraments, except Holy Orders, which is reserved to the Bishop.

Religious Priest

Man of faith and prayer living in a community of other men who share his spiritual commitments. Priestly ministry may include teaching, missionary work overseas, social work, or chaplain assignments. Vows involve poverty, chastity, and obedience to his religious superiors and the Church. Minister of the sacraments, except Holy Orders.

Religious Brother or Sister

Man or woman of faith and prayer, committed to live in a religious

community with others. May work in service to others as a nurse, teacher, counselor, social worker, or administrator, or may serve others through a life of contemplative prayer. Vows are poverty, chastity, and obedience.

Member of Secular Institute

Man or woman belonging to an institute of consecrated life made up of single laypersons and/or members of the clergy. Laypersons retain their occupations in life. Vows involve poverty, chastity, and obedience professed within the institute rather than publicly. Members strive for the perfection of charity and work for the sanctification of the world.

Permanent Deacon

Man of faith and prayer, single or married, called to serve the Church through the ordained diaconate, often in addition to his professional work. Assists priests and bishop by preaching and baptizing and witnessing marriages. A deacon who is married must be at least thirty-five years old and have the consent of his wife.

Married Person

Man or woman of faith and prayer called to live in a covenant partnership toward the good of the spouse and the procreation and education of children. Involves a general call to the vocation of marriage and a specific call to another as a life partner. Vow of fidelity to each other through the sacrament of matrimony.

Single Person (Called)

Man or woman of faith called to live a celibate single life, not committed to another person or to the consecrated religious life. The person may even be consecrated to perpetual chastity—a celibate life.

Single Person (Pre-Vocational)

Man or woman of faith and prayer seeking God's will for his vocation and particular state of life. All begin life as single persons, called to live in chastity while listening for God's call.

Lay Positions in the Catholic Church

There are also many occupations a lay person (single or married) can pursue in service to the Church, such as the following:

Director of Religious Education

Youth Director

Social Services Worker

Music Director

Administrator

Secretary

Marriage, Family, and Child Counselor

Volunteer work within the church setting is also open to single and married lay people.

Lector

Extraordinary Minister of the Eucharist

Cantor

Musician/Choir Member

Religious Education Teacher

Youth Leader

Catholic Scout Leader

Parish Council Member

Usher

Missionaries are lay men and women (as well as priests, brothers, and sisters) called to serve others, through Christ, in the world. This service brings God's love, healing, kindness, and hope in a mission established by the Church within one's own country or overseas.

All of these activities bear witness to living the gospel and serving others in love.

Vows—What Are They?

What do vows in the religious life involve?

The vow of poverty

Letting go of all possessions, sharing all in common, and serving the poor; putting aside expectations and concern for the opinion of others.

The vow of chastity

Living a life of consecrated celibacy or virginity; loving universally, with intimacy and friendships founded spiritually in love.

The vow of obedience

Following the will of God as it is expressed through a rule of life approved by the Church, and the direction of the religious superior.

For More Information

There are a number of other avenues to which a Catholic may be called, such as membership in a third order.

For further information on a religious vocation, contact:

1. Your diocesan Vocations Director or parish priest.

2. National Coalition for Church Vocations (NCCV)
   1603 South Michigan Avenue, Suite 400
   Chicago, Illinois 60016
   (312) 663–5453
   1–800–671–NCCV

Resources

Catholic Resources for Further Reading

Faith

The Angel and the Ants: Bringing Heaven Closer to Your Daily Life. Peter Kreeft. Ann Arbor: Servant Books, 1994.

Simply outstanding! Profound wisdom for everyday life written in Kreeft's usual witty style. Hard to put this one down. 196 pages.

————

Catholic and Christian. Alan Schreck. Ann Arbor: Servant Books, 1984.

Outstanding review and exploration of commonly misunderstood Catholic beliefs, including salvation, source of Catholic beliefs, the Pope, sacraments, saints, Mary, and leadership in the Body of Christ. 232 pages.

————

The Catholic Answer Book. Peter M. J. Stravinskas. Huntington, Ind.: Our Sunday Visitor, 1990.

Contains answers to frequently asked questions concerning the Catholic faith. Well done. 192 pages.

The Catholic Answer Book 2. Peter M. J. Stravinskas. Huntington, Ind.: Our Sunday Visitor, 1990.

More of the same. 238 pages.

————

Catholicism and Fundamentalism: The Attack on "Romanism" by "Bible Christians". Karl Keating. San Francisco: Ignatius Press, 1988.

An incredibly strong defense of Catholicism against attacks by fundamentalists. 360 pages.

————

Father McBride's Teen Catechism. Alfred McBride, O. Praem. Huntington, Ind.: Our Sunday Visitor, 1995.

Presentation of the Catholic faith for teenagers based on the Catechism. 183 pages.

————

The Holy Bible, Revised Standard Version, Catholic Edition. San Francisco: Ignatius Press (Thomas Nelson & Sons, publisher), © 1965, 1966.

The Old and New Testaments in a superb translation.

Introduction to Mary: The Heart of Marian Doctrine and Devotion. Mark Miravalle. Santa Barbara: Queenship Publishing Company, 1993.

Answers questions about Mary, including the Catholic response to ten common objections to Marian doctrine and devotion. 193 pages.

Proud to Be Catholic. Fr. Kenneth J. Roberts. Huntington, Ind.: Our Sunday Visitor Publishing Division, 1995.

Straightforward, easy-to-read book explaining essentials of the Catholic faith. 126 pages.

We're on a Mission from God. Mary Beth Bonacci. San Francisco: Ignatius Press, 1996.

A wonderful book for young people on the Catholic faith and their role in the Church. 215 pages.

What Catholics Really Believe— Setting the Record Straight. Karl Keating. San Francisco: Ignatius Press, 1992.

Contains 52 answers to common misconceptions about the Catholic faith. 155 pages.

What Does God Want? A Practical Guide to Making Decisions. Michael Scanlan, T.O.R., with James Manney. Huntington, Ind.: Our Sunday Visitor Publishing Division, 1996.

Offers a five-part approach for Godly decision making, based on Catholic tradition and Fr. Scanlan's over thirty years of experience in spiritual direction, counseling, and teaching. 127 pages.

Yes or No: Straight Answers to Tough Questions about Christianity. Peter Kreeft. San Francisco: Ignatius Press, 1991.

Using a dialogue between Sal the Seeker and Chris the Christian, many of the gospel's mysteries are approached in an engaging manner. Good reading for youth and adults! 191 pages.

Your Questions, God's Answers. Peter Kreeft. San Francisco: Ignatius Press, 1994.

A book for young people. Through the use of Scripture, answers are provided to the most significant questions asked by youth. 121 pages.

Family

The Book of Virtues. William J. Bennett. New York: Simon and Schuster, 1993.

What more can be said about this phenomenal book? It is a treasure chest of stories on morality spanning the virtues of self-discipline, compassion, responsibility, friendship, work, and much more. An absolute must for every family. 831 pages.

―――――

Bringing Christ's Presence into Your Home: Your Family as a Domestic Church. Keith Fournier. Nashville: Thomas Nelson, 1992.

An excellent book for bringing Christ into the center of family life. 227 pages.

―――――

A Guide for the Study of Familiaris Consortio: The Community of the Family. William F. Maestri. Boston: St. Paul Books and Media, 1995.

Commentary on Pope John Paul II's encyclical on The Christian Family in the Modern World. 103 pages.

―――――

The Heart of Virtue. Donald de Marco. San Francisco: Ignatius Press, 1996.

A presentation of twenty-eight virtues and related stories. 231 pages.

―――――

Life with Joseph. Rev. Paul J. Gormon. St. Paul, Minn.: The Leaflet Missal Company, 1988.

A great little book on the life of St. Joseph. Many applications to daily living are given based on the holiness of this great man. 96 pages.

―――――

Love and Family. Mercedes Arzú Wilson. San Francisco: Ignatius Press, 1996.

A comprehensive resource for parents on family issues. Many practical suggestions. Illustrated. 383 pages.

―――――

The Moral Compass. William J. Bennett. New York: Simon and Schuster, 1995.

Companion to the *Book of Virtues* drawing upon great literature and stories from history. 824 pages.

―――――

The New Wine—Christian Witness of the Family. Carlo Maria Martini. Boston: St. Paul Books and Media, 1994.

Various family topics by Cardinal Martini, Archbishop of Milan, including family prayer, television, work, vocation, and educating children in the Faith. 319 pages.

———

Only Heroic Catholic Families Will Survive. Fr. Robert J. Fox. Alexandria, S. Dak.: Family Apostolate, 1994.

Another collection of essays by excellent Catholic writers on the survival of the Catholic family through the interrelationship with the Catholic faith in Jesus Christ. Good section on vocations. 296 pages.

———

Talking to Your Children about Being Catholic. Huntington, Ind.: Our Sunday Visitor, 1991.

A collection of nine essays offering good explanations of Church teaching on many subjects. 141 pages.

———

The Truth and Meaning of Human Sexuality—Guidelines for Education within the Family. Pontifical Council for the Family. Boston: St. Paul Books and Media, 1996.

Guidance and suggestions in support of parents teaching their children about human sexuality. Must reading. 95 pages.

———

Prayer

Appointment with God. Michael Scanlan, T.O.R. Steubenville, Ohio: Franciscan University Press, 1987.

Very useful book on prayer using a five-stage process. Especially helpful for those who lack time for prayer or are struggling with how to pray. Recommended for teenage to adult years. 57 pages.

———

Father Peyton's Rosary Prayer Book. Albany, N.Y.: The Family Rosary, 1984.

A wonderful book on the mysteries of the rosary. "The family that prays together, stays together." 218 pages.

———

Father Roberts' Guide to Personal Prayer. Fr. Kenneth Roberts. Huntington, Ind.: Our Sunday Visitor, 1992.

A great little booklet on prayer. 22 pages.

———

A Prayer Book for Young Catholics. Fr. Robert J. Fox, Huntington, Ind.: Our Sunday Visitor, 1981.

Many useful prayers suitable for teenagers and young adults. 168 pages.

Saints

Modern Saints: Their Lives and Faces. 2 vols. Ann Ball. Rockford, Ill.: Tan Books and Publishers, 1983.

Thorough, well-illustrated book covering saints mostly from the 1800s through the 1900s. 458 and 510 pages.

———

The One Year Book of Saints. Rev. Clifford Stevens. Huntington, Ind.: Our Sunday Visitor Publishing Division, 1989.

Saints for each month of the year, including a thought for the day and a Bible selection. 383 pages.

———

Saints and Other Powerful Men in the Church. Bob and Penny Lord. Journeys of Faith, 1990.

Many excellent chapters on saints such as John Bosco, Francis of Assisi, Augustine, as well as other men like Padre Pio and Archbishop Fulton J. Sheen. 527 pages.

———

Saints and Other Powerful Women in the Church. Bob and Penny Lord. Journeys of Faith, 1994.

Like the book on men, well written with black and white photographs covering saints such as Clare of Assisi, Teresa of Avila, Catherine of Siena,

plus Mother Angelica, Sister Briege McKenna, and others. 396 pages.

———

Secular Saints. Joan Carrol Cruz. Rockford, Ill.: Tan Books and Publishers, 1989.

Easy-to-read biographies of 250 canonized and beatified laymen, women, and children. Black and white illustrations and photographs. 780 pages.

———

Vocation

Called by God—A Theology of Vocation and Life-Long Commitment. Marie Theresa Coombs and Francis Kelly Nemeck. Collegeville, Minn.: The Liturgical Press, 1992.

Theological study of the mystery of vocation and God's will. 153 pages.

———

Discerning Vocations to Marriage, Celibacy, and Singlehood. Marie Theresa Coombs and Francis Kelly Nemeck. Collegeville, Minn.: The Liturgical Press, 1994.

Excellent adult-level book on the vocational core of marriage, celibacy, and the single life. 217 pages.

———

Let Us Pray for Vocations. Fr. Enzo Buccheri. North Hills, Calif.:

Harvest Prayer Association for Vocations, 1992.

Excellent book of prayers for vocations by the Congregation of Rogationists. 160 pages.

———

Playboy to Priest. Rev. Kenneth Roberts. Huntington, Ind.: Our Sunday Visitor, 1973.

Great book about God's call in the life of Fr. Roberts. Fun to read! Highly recommended. 297 pages.

———

Priest, Sister, Brother, Deacon, and You. Chicago, Ill.: National Coalition for Church Vocations.

Questions often asked by high-school students about Church vocations. Many more resources like this are available from the National Coalition for Church Vocations. Booklet, 15 pages.

———

A Religious Vocation: Is It for Me? Rev. Martin W. Pable. Huntington, Ind.: Our Sunday Visitor, 1988.

Well-written booklet about God's call and personal vocation. Appropriate for those considering religious or lay choices. 46 pages.

———

The Pope

By John Paul II. Boston: Pauline Books and Media.

Highly recommended letters from the Holy Father on matters of family, vocation, work, and the life of Mary and Joseph.

Consecrated Life (Vita Consecrata). March 25, 1996.

I Will Give You Shepherds (Pastores Dabo Vobis). March 25, 1992.

"Letter of the Pope to Children in the Year of the Family." December 13, 1994.

"Letter to Families from Pope John Paul II." February 2, 1994.

Mother of the Redeemer (Redemptoris Mater). March 25, 1987.

On the Dignity and Vocation of Women (Mulieris Dignitatem). August 15, 1988.

Guardian of the Redeemer: On the Person and Mission of Saint Joseph (Redemptoris Custos). August 15, 1989.

The Role of the Christian Family in the Modern World (Familiaris Consortio). November 22, 1981.

The Vocation and the Mission of the Lay Faithful in the Church and in the World (Christifideles Laici). December 30, 1988.

Career Reference Books

America's 50 Fastest Growing Jobs: The Authoritative Information Source. Indianapolis: JIST Works, 1994.

Contains detailed job descriptions for the fifty fastest growing jobs based on U.S. Department of Labor information. High-school to adult level. 232 pages.

———

America's Top 300 Jobs: A Complete Career Handbook. Indianapolis: JIST Works, 1994.

Based on the Occupational Outlook Handbook, with additional material, such as employment trends projected to 2005. Best for high-school to adult level. 525 pages.

———

Career Emphasis Series. JIST Works, 1990.

Offers four title useful in career planning:

Making Good Decisions (techniques for career planning). 73 pages.

Understanding Yourself (identifying interests, skills, values, and life-style preferences). 59 pages.

Preparing for Work (goal-setting, education and training options, skills for positive outcome). 57 pages.

Getting a Good Job and Getting Ahead (approaches to finding employment and adjusting to change). 81 pages.

———

Children's Dictionary of Occupations. William Hopke and Barbara Parramore. Bloomington, Ill.: Meridian Education Corporation, 1992.

Contains over 300 occupations in a simplified form most suitable for elementary school but useful at the intermediate-school level also. Separate section describing fourteen jobs for teenagers. 130 pages.

———

Children's Occupational Outlook Handbook. Auburn, Calif.: CFKR Career Materials, 1995.

Simplified version of the Occupational Outlook Handbook and the Student's Occupational Outlook Handbook.

Contains 190 occupations arranged within eleven groups, plus seven occupations listed under a "Youth Jobs" category. Well done and best for elementary and intermediate school. 219 pages.

———

College Costs & Financial Aid Handbook, 1996 Edition. New York: College Entrance Examination Board, 1995.

Current costs, financial aid information, and other facts on 2,800 accredited colleges, plus index of colleges that offer academic, music, drama, art, or athletic scholarships. Very useful book for college planners. 329 pages.

———

The Complete Guide for Occupational Exploration. Indianapolis: JIST Works, 1993.

An easy-to-use guide with over 12,000 jobs arranged in twelve major interest clusters. Very worthwhile for students, parents, teachers, career changers, guidance specialists, and job seekers. High school to adult. Huge book! 915 pages.

———

Dictionary of Occupational Titles, Volumes I and II. U.S. Department of Labor, Employment, and Training Administration, 1991.

Mega-book containing over 12,000 job descriptions, covering nearly every type of occupation in the United States. Revised and updated (previous edition was published in 1977). Distributed by JIST Works, Inc., Indianapolis, Ind. 1,404 pages.

———

Exploring Careers: A Young Person's Guide to Over 300 Jobs. Indianapolis: JIST Works, 1990.

Contains information on over 300 jobs, including a self-guided career interest survey. Best for high-school level. 462 pages. A companion 32-page student workbook and 113-page instructor's guide are also available.

———

The 1995 What Color Is Your Parachute: A Practical Manual for Job-Hunters & Career-Changers. Richard Bolles. Berkeley, Calif.: Ten Speed Press, 1995.

Great reading, especially in the post-high-school, young-adult years or for adult midlife career changes. Covers job hunting, choosing or changing a career, and job interviewing. Extensive appendix on finding your mission in life, locating a career counselor, and finding additional resources. 480 pages.

———

Occupational Outlook Handbook. U.S. Department of Labor, Bureau of Labor Statistics, 1996–1997 edition.

Outstanding reference source describing about 250 occupations in twelve major groups, which covers about 104 million jobs, or 85 percent of all jobs in the United States. Covers employment outlook, training requirements, nature of the work, earnings, and sources to contact for additional information. Produced in even years by the U.S. Department of Labor, Bureau of Labor Statistics. 505 pages.

————

Student's Occupational Outlook Handbook. Auburn, Calif.: CFKR Career Materials, 1995.

Simplified version of the *Occupational Outlook Handbook* for middle and high-school levels. Covers about three hundred occupations arranged in twenty-seven groups. Includes skills needed, training, working conditions, nature of the work, growth, earnings, and sources of additional information. Excellent resource. 283 pages.

Young Person's Occupational Outlook Handbook. Indianapolis: JIST Works, 1996.

Another simplified approach to the *Occupational Outlook Handbook* offering descriptions for the top 250 jobs in the United States. Contains information about the job duties, working conditions, related jobs, sources of additional information, and related school subjects. Appropriate for grades five through nine. 262 pages.

————